Take a Pause, Paul

A Book about Commas

library washrooms gym lockers playground

by Marie Powell
illustrated by Anthony Lewis

amicus readers

3

Say Hello to Amicus Readers.

You'll find our helpful dog, Amicus, chasing a ball—to let you know the reading level of a book.

1
Learn to Read
Frequent repetition, high frequency words, and close photo-text matches introduce familiar topics and provide support for brand new readers.

2
Read Independently
Some repetition is mixed with varied sentence structures and a select amount of new vocabulary words are introduced with text and photo support.

3
Read to Know More
Interesting facts and engaging art and photos give fluent readers fun books both for reading practice and to learn about new topics.

Amicus Readers are published by Amicus
P.O. Box 1329, Mankato, MN 56002
www.amicuspublishing.us

Illustrations by Anthony Lewis

Produced for Amicus by The Peterson Publishing Company and Red Line Editorial.

Editor Jenna Gleisner
Designer Jake Nordby

Printed in Malaysia
10 9 8 7 6 5 4 3 2 1

Library of Congress Cataloging-in-Publication Data
Powell, Marie, 1958-
 Take a pause, Paul : a book about commas / by Marie Powell ; Illustrations by Anthony Lewis.
   pages cm. -- (Punctuation station)
 "Paul excitedly shows Mya around her new school, while both learn how to correctly use commas in a sentence."
 Audience: K to Grade 3.
 ISBN 978-1-60753-731-1 (library binding)
 ISBN 978-1-60753-835-6 (ebook)
 1. Comma--Juvenile literature. 2. English language--Punctuation--Juvenile literature. I. Lewis, Anthony, 1966 illustrator. II. Title. III. Title: Book about commas.
 PE1450.P67 2015
 428.1'3--dc23
                                    2014045810

Punctuation marks help us understand writing. Commas show where to pause in a sentence.

After moving with her family, Mya is starting at a new school.

Ms. Tate asks Paul to show Mya around the school.

"Paul, please make a list of the places you would like to show Mya," says Ms. Tate.

I will show Mya the library washrooms gym lockers and playground and I will show her our class pets.

"What are the library washrooms? Can we go see the gym lockers first?" asks Mya.

"Take a pause, Paul," says Ms. Tate. "Remember your commas."

"Oh right! The library, washrooms, gym, lockers, and playground are all separate places. I've added a comma between each place," says Paul.

I will show Mya the library, washrooms, gym, lockers, and playground and I will show our class pets.

9

I will show Mya the library, washrooms, gym, lockers, and playground, and I will show her our class pets.

"Take another pause, Paul. Are you forgetting one more comma?" asks Ms. Tate.

"I almost forgot! This is two sentences, but I've added a pause now," says Paul. "Does this help, Mya?" asks Paul.

"The list doesn't seem so long now. I think I can remember all of the places," says Mya.

the library,
...kers, and playground,
...class pets.

13

"I'll help you, and I'll introduce you to everyone!" says Paul. "After I show you around, you can see our pet gerbil, hamster, and snake!"

Remember to use a comma:

To separate words at the beginning of a sentence:
After moving with her family, Mya is starting at a new school.

To separate items in a list:
The library, washrooms, gym, lockers, and playground are all separate places.

To connect sentences with words such as "and":
I'll help you, and I'll introduce you to everyone!